JEAN NOUVEL

JEAN NOUVEL

Marco Casamonti

Motta

Jean Nouvel

Cover
Institut du Monde Arabe, Paris
Photo
© Georges Fessy, Parigi

Translation
Clarice Zdanski

minimum
essential architecture library

Series edited by Giovanni Leoni

Published Titles

Mario Botta
Santiago Calatrava
Richard Meier
Rafael Moneo
Pier Luigi Nervi
Renzo Piano
Álvaro Siza

For the excerpts reproduced in the sections
"Thought" and "Critique," the authors and publishers
wish to thank those who have authorised their
publication. The publisher is available for any queries
regarding sections for which it has not been possible
to trace the holder of the rights.

© 2008 Il Sole 24 ORE Business Media srl, Milan
© 2009 24 ORE Motta Cultura srl, Milan
© 2009 Il Sole 24 ORE Business Media srl, Milan

First Italian Edition: March 2008
First English Edition: October 2009

ISBN: 978-88-6413-013-2

Printed in Italy

Contents

Portfolio

Introduction

Nouvel – The Architecture

By a new literary coincidence, new – that is, *nouveau* in French – becomes *nouvel* when placed before a vowel or a mute "h". Thus in the mixture of languages, when in transalpine grammar 'new' is placed before the word architecture, which in most languages is written with "a" (even though in French, it takes the feminine suffix "-le"), it phonetically coincides with the surname of the author generally know as the most attentive interpreter of future or futurable scenarios. Nevertheless, Nouvel's *Nouvelle Architecture*, or to be exact, the new architecture of the French architect, might appear to us as such because, leaving aside the commonplaces of a superficial reading, it constantly goes beyond the idea of time by compressing past, present and future into a single act that appears – and is – of necessity contemporary, where contemporary assumes the literal value of what happens, takes place, lives and works in the same period of time that for Nouvel must be represented in the project.

It is a question of taking action and composing, for this reason so seductive, where tradition and innovation, artifice and naturalness, shiny and opaque are intermingled continually, in an skilful alternation of co-presences, and blended by a careful director who suddenly makes all of the categories used up to now obsolete and unserviceable, to set apart fashions and trends in architecture. Therefore, the ultra-modern sequence of diaphragms that hydraulically regulate the solar irradiation in the well-known Institut du Monde Arabe would only be a sterile mechanism of vaguely High-Tech automation if he had not sublimely interpreted the geometry and decorative apparatus of a cultural neighbourhood where tradition withdraws, as in a Persian rug, into an infinite succession of figures that range from the square to the circle to the star of David. In the same way, the technological covering of the opera house in Lyon would be nothing if its plan and profile were not included in an evolutionary chain that began with the Renaissance Palladian reconstruction of the decrepit Palazzo della Ragione in Vicenza: the "basilica", to the Neo-classical metallic arcades of Joseph Paxton's Crystal Palace.

And again, how can we read the pointed profiles of the pitch roofs of the bodies of the Hotel Saint James in Bordeaux if not as an attempt to represent, through a simple grid of corten steel, the complex urban articulation of French rural villages, or how can we understand the meaning and value of the vegetal façades of the Musée du Quai Branly in Paris if not as the expression of a will towards the hybridisation of artificial urban landscape and the natural image of a rustic landscape that the garden and the forest contend for?

Nouvel's architecture feeds on these dualities that then become triads of references, or multiple references that are difficult to count, eluding any sort of attempt at the homologation e that is so convenient to the synthesis of historians, while it provides original nourishment to the gaze of architects who, in that way of working, seek not so much a shortcut for formal emulation, as the experience of research and experimentation that is the distinctive characteristic of a varied and unpredictable way of working.

For these reasons, Nouvel shows an evident aversion towards critical cataloguing of his achievement and his work, if not for belonging to the modernity that he himself declares as an immanent and ineliminable fact – not a style, or calligraphy, but a way of being and participating in collective life and in one's own present. Modernity, said Nouvel in the course of one of his famous lectures held at the Milan Triennale on 8 April 1996, "is the best use of our memory and the greatest energy, the strongest push forward in the sense of an evolution the can be received", and it is to this capacity for continuous modification that he feels the architect should cling as his specific task – a task that goes beyond time, history, historicism and the labels that many have tried to place on him. Again, in the course of the same lecture, as on many other public occasions, Nouvel's *incipit* moves from a stipulation that coincides with the refusal to be remembered as a High-Tech architect. But all the same, we could say this in the face of any sort of stylistic paradigm, since his works could be read at times as minimalist, for example in the simple volumes of the Génoscope built in Lanaud, Limousin, in 1994, at others as a case of formal

Pierre et Vacances,
Cap d'Ail

subject of an action taken, which always goes back to the construction of a state of mind and an emotion for which he foresees and feeds multiple sequences of reactions. Nevertheless, in the French architect's kaleidoscopic way of working, everything does not have the same weight or the same value, and there is no trace of formal digression or ambiguous eclecticism, since in the alterity of the different scenes, there emerges a coherent and constant search for the interpretation of the text and the con-text.

So, for the sake of simplicity in reading, let's try to identify and underline the cornerstones of a multilateral way of thinking, understanding the result of the author's architecture through his name, and in "adjectivising" him, the meaning of his work in relation to individual interpretative hypotheses.

Nouvel and the Context

In every form of architecture, in every project, designed simply, in progress or already constructed, there emerges evident attention to contingent facts, expressed as the interpretation of a place, of a state of mind or, more simply, as a story that can add a different point of observation to what exists. As a consequence, Nouvel's reading and restoring is never neutral, nor mimetic; it is never reductive of a reality that appears changed and different each time, positively altered by a regenerating action that, even though born of the context, elaborates a new, spectacular and seductive version. Undoubtedly Nouvel succeeds in discerning in every urban matter the essence of things and of the landscape that, full of history as it might be, appears as stripped of any form of historicism, and although full of modernity, is never translated into a flight towards oblivion freed from any sort of pre-existing suggestion. This is probably why Eric Lapierre dedicated a book entitled *Love Context* to Nouvel's work where he underlines how his buildings are the result of an encounter between personal poetics centred on the perception of the senses and the value of a place whose value and characteristics can be gathered and heightened.

For these reasons, insists Lapierre, each one of Jean Nouvel's buildings is different from the other, and that is why each project is a new project, a different interpretation of the role and aims of the

maximalism – just think of the eclectic Musée du Quai Branly concluded in 2006, or as a particular expression of the post-modern suspended between technicism and classicism, as demonstrate the different visions in plan and elevation of the recently built Guthrie Theater in Minneapolis. The truth is that Nouvel, as a creator of images, is all of this together. He is the inclusive co-presence of what history makes available to him, both from the typological distributive point of view and from the technical and constructive point of view, and as repertory of forms and models used indistinctly according to a narrative will that crosses the borders of the discipline of architecture to land in other worlds and ways of representation, from theatre to the cinema, from writing to music and evidently to the visual arts. The tools he uses, from technology to history, from genetic manipulation to geometry, never constitute the essence or the

Euralille, Lille

architectural project, a project that always defines its own individual specificity.

As Nouvel himself has maintained, it is a question of "acute and opportunist" architecture that does not submit to any formal rule written *a priori*, and that tries to seize from every occasion the nourishment and energy of its own way of constructing itself.

Nouvel and History

Inasmuch as what has been stated above might make evident a parallel between Le Corbusier's work and the critical action brought about by Nouvel's architecture, since in both authors, even though with decades of distance between them, adhesion to modernity does not exclude active participation in history considered as a tool of knowledge of the present and of opening towards future scenarios. No concession to nostalgia, no concession to memory, no retrospective complacency, if not as an act of investigation from which to draw creative impulses that might change the already known, and set off towards new opportunities – new, in fact, not in the abstract sense, but new because the difference is measured against the previous condition. It is a matter of a vision and an active conception of the role of history and of the time that carries it, as in the case of the corner building of the Galeries Lafayette in Berlin, to interpret the urban role of the construction considered as an occasion to respect and at the same time change the specific condition of the architecture of the city. The building consciously embodies a totally neoclassical whole, equipped with a base, cornice and inclined roof. It

Hotel Saint James,
Bordeaux

Opposite page
Cultural Centre, Lucerne

does not reject the singular condition that makes it a monument and cornerstone of the street. Nevertheless, it shrinks from any sort of historicist interpretation, making itself evanescent to observation, transparent with respect to darkness and reflecting during daytime hours, to the point of setting off, amidst the vitreous surfaces of the wrapping, a play of mirrors and multiple visions that cross the space, enlivening it and making it spectacular.

Nouvel and Modernity

According to a dynamic conception of modernity, not identified in a set historical period but rather considered as the constant of a propositional attitude that crosses time and its different seasons, we can say with certainty that Nouvel, above and beyond his own statements, is an intimately modern architect, which coincides with his participation in the modernity of Brunelleschi and Alberti, with the perspectival innovation introduced by Borromini and

Scharoun, with the support of technology as introduced by Eiffel and Le Corbusier. However, it also reflects and crosses the classicism of Mies and the refined use decoration as introduced by Frank Lloyd Wright – as an emblematic case of this last theme, it is worth mentioning the vision of the project currently in progress for the office building tower in Doha in Quatar.

For Nouvel, modernity is a constant action of research that has nothing of the formal, that is not read in the play of illuminated white volumes; it does not allude to the construction of a style, but to the affirmation of a system of aesthetics that is considered inclusive of all the images and suggestions of past contemporariness, and through their composition and hybridisation, of the future.

Nouvel and the Arts

In accordance with what Olivier Boissière has written we can, in fact, recognize that Nouvel's way of working coincides with a conception of

aesthetics that includes and uses many contemporary expressive modes, whether they be taken from the world of the visual arts or from industrial production, from science, from the cinema or from photography. Nouvel's aesthetics, however, does not use the instrument of collage, but rather selects genres and icons that appear each time as the most appropriate to express the value of his thought by raising in the spectator those sensations sought in the project through the use of hyperrealist images. Of course, many artists, from Joseph Beuys to Walter De Maria, from Donald Judd to Richard Serra, or from Federico Fellini to Wim Wenders, have attracted and contaminated his way of observing reality always restored with clearly narrative insistence. In this feverish yet sublime search for images, Nouvel puts himself forward as an artist in the complete sense of the term, a composer of visions, a director who lives architecture as the expression of inhabiting that is a concentration of emotions and diversified experiences. Consequently, the universe of art attracts him as an instrumental opportunity for a way of building that needs, consumes and reverberates a multitude of images and materials that are never so much exclusive or repeated as they are original and diversified according to specific accumulations and stratifications.

Nouvel and the Cinema

As an architect, Nouvel does not use the rigid methodological sequence of designing everything inside the discipline, but rather, the intuition and agility of the film director who uses his time and work in constructing images and sequences rendered inhabitable by necessity. In fact, the instruments used belong not so much to the static construction of property that we usually define as "fixed or immovable", as to the dynamic dimension of living, where the composition of the whole is constituted of frameworks full of contrasts, of light and shade, of continuous, unpredictable changes in scale and takes, from below to on high, from the interior towards the exterior, from the material towards the immaterial. Nouvel enriches his architectural images with real images, with projections, with reflections, while the scene or the architectural narration never excludes photography or construction from the frame. This conception of construction is celebrated with the

Fondation Cartier, built in Paris between 1991 and 1994, when the architect suggested destroying an old stone wall running along the Boulevard Raspail and replacing it with a screen of glass that would not only restore but also amplify and frame the view of the park. The building is not only a space that contains, but also the views it proposes, since the trees and plants are reflected and refracted like the external lights of the avenue and the people that enliven it on the inside, according to life going on, like an infinite feature film. The theme thus crosses the border of the simple idea of transparency, going into a zone of multi-vision marked by the passing of days and the alternating of colour and images that change from dawn to dusk, with the changing of time, reflecting the clouds as well as dazzling sunlight.

Moreover, as in the art of the cinema, Nouvel gathers the idea of the plot, from which he translates expedients and typological innovations useful for leading the multiple images that make up his special way of composing back to unity. His architecture often needs an underlying theme, something leading back to unity, a reference to a unifying subject, as happens with the use of great protruding coverings: this is the case with the conference centre in Lucerne or in the extension of the Regina Sofia museum in Madrid, where the contemporary fragmented and unitary nature of the two buildings ends up in a particular overall frame that can identify, both a new relationship between the landscape and the water of the lake, as well as a skilful mending of the urban fabric.

Nouvel and Nature

With respect to the contamination between nature and architecture, even if it would be more suitable to speak of botany applied to the world of construction, it was a fatal event when Nouvel met Patrick Blanc, a researcher at the Centre National de la Recherche Scientifique and head of the tropical plant biology laboratory at the Université Pierre et Marie Curie, with whom he started a series of experiments with "green" architecture characterised by the presence of garden-walls and park-surfaces. For the French architect, the possibility of fusing architecture and nature meant opening a new, boundless chapter in terms of technology, of images and of the quality of habitation, not to mention opening completely

unexpected typological and constructional fronts. Nouvel's proposals, for the Musée du Quai Branly, as well as for the vegetal tower in Kuala Lumpur, have nothing of the romantic or decadent, but rather aim for the re-naturalization of the constructed landscape, for the creation of new volumetric urban parks, for the identification of changeable surfaces equipped with a vitality of their own.

The innovation, from a technical point of view, lies in the possibility of using vegetal material, plants that can grow without soil, and take root in specially designed humidified felt. Windows seem to be frames for pictures surrounded by plant material, a living, changing iridescent substance that changes with the passing of time, making the architecture seem as though it belongs to the world of animate beings.

Leeum Samsung Museum, Seoul

Chronology

1945	Born in Fumel in France
1966	Passed admissions examination for the Ecole Nationale Supérieure des Beaux-Arts
1967	Became the assistant of Claude Parent and Paul Virilio (until 1970)
1970	Won the competition "Site naturel création architecturale" Formed a partnership with François Seigneur (until 1972)
1972	Took his degree at the Ecole Nationale Supérieure des Beaux-Arts Entered into a partnership with Gilbert Lézénès and François Seigneur (until 1981)
1973	Delbigot residence, Villeneuve sur Lot
1974	Delanghe residential complex, Perigueux Nursery school, Trelissac
1976	Co-founder of *Mars 1976* (French architectural movement) Media library and library at the Trocadero, Paris
1977	Co-founder of *Syndacat de l'Architecture* Contributed to the organization of the international competition for the Les Halles area, Paris
1978	Founder and artistic consultant for the Biennial of Architecture at the Paris Biennial
1979	Clinic, Bezons Devoldere residence, Troyes
1980	CES Anne Frank, Antony
1981	Won the competition for the Institut du Monde Arabe, the first in a series of grand-scale projects put forward by the head of the government François Mitterrand Formed a partnership with Gilbert Lézénès and Pierre Soria (until 1984)
1982	SEA Center, Kerjouanno Ministry of Finance, Paris (project never carried out) La Villette park, Paris (project never carried out)
1983	Received the Silver Medal of the Académie d'Architecture Awarded a *laurea Honoris Causa* from the University of Buenos Aires Universal Expo, Paris Offices of Yves Dauges Concert hall, Bagnolet
1984	Theater, Belfort Media library, Nîmes In Paris, founded Jean Nouvel et Associés (Jean Nouvel, Jean-Marc Ibos, Myrto Vitart, Emmanuel Blamont, until 1989) Foundation of JNEC (Jean Nouvel and Emmanuel Cattani, until 1994)
1986	Sports centre, Nîmes Gymnase du Luzard, Marne la Vallée
1987	Won the prize for the best French building of the year with the project for the Institut du Monde Arabe (carried out in 1989) Exhibit "Jean Nouvel, Architectures d'art et d'essai" at the Institut Français d'Architecture in Paris and Nîmes Residential complex, Saint Ouen Dhuoda, Nîmes

	Neumausus, Nîmes
	La Coupole, Combs la Ville
1988	Palais de Tokyo, Paris
	Musée Rodin, Paris
	Beaubourg - Années 50, Paris
	Onyx, Saint Herblain
	Gallerie Bailly, Paris
1989	Won the Agha Khan prize for the project for the Institut du Monde Arabe in Paris
	La Défense, Paris (competition project)
	Institut du Monde Arabe
	French Pavilion at the Universal Expo in Seville
	Hotel Saint James, Bouillac
	Bailly Apartments, Paris
	ADP Offices, Paris
	INIST, Nancy
1990	Received the Architectural Record prize for the project for the Hotel Saint Jamesin Bouillac
	Exhibit "Jean Nouvel, architecte", Tours
	Exhibit "Jean Nouvel, Opere Recenti 1987-1990", Palazzo Lanfranchi, Pisa
	"Jean Nouvel, Das werk eines Pariser architekten" at the Studio Dumont in Köln
	Palazzo del Cinema, Venice (competition project)
	Interdica, Freiburg
1991	Exhibit "Jean Nouvel & Emmanuel Cattani et associés" at the ETH in Zurich
	Installation of the exhibit of Georges Boudaille, Paris
	Pierre et Vacances block of flats, Cap D'Ail
	Poulain, Blois
1992	Exhibit "La metropole selon Jean Nouvel", Tostem Spacelab, Tokyo
	Exhibit "Nouvel", Institute of Contemporary Arts, London
	Hotel des Thermes, Dax
	Perception, Herouville Saint Clair
	CLMBBDO, Issy les Moulineaux
	Bus stop, Tours
1993	Received a prize from the American Institute of Architecture in Chicago for the project for the
	Opéra in Lyon as the best French building of the year
	Exhibit "Jean Nouvel", Bordeaux
	Sac Parmentier, Bezons
	L'Opéra, Lyon
	Musée Gallo-Roman, Perigueux
	Cartier CTL, Saint Imier
	Church of Sainte Marie, Sarlat
	Block of flats, Tours
	Parking building, Tours
	Tourist Office, Tours
	Conference centre, Tours
1994	Founded the Ateliers Jean Nouvel with Michel Pélissié
	Fondation Cartier, Paris
	Social centre, Herouville Saint Clair
	Génoscope, Paris
1995	Granted recognition by RIBA (Royal Institute of British Architecture)
	Galeries Lafayette, Berlin
	Euralille, Lille
	La Villette park – Mesure Démesure, Paris

1997 Exhibit "Jean Nouvel Architectures", Fundaçaõ Armando Alvares Penteado, Saõ Pauo
Received recognition Commandeur de l'Ordre des Arts et des Lettres
H-Project, Seoul

1998 Awarded the Gold Medal by the Académie d'Architecture
Exhibit "Jean Nouvel, Architecture Store", Store Front Gallery, New York
Opera House, Beijing (competition project)
Musée de la Publicité, Paris

1999 Interunfall, Bregenz
Expansion of the Museo Nacional Centro de Arte Reina Sofia, Madrid
Musée du Quai Branly, Paris (carried out in 2006)
Fondation Cognac-Jay, Rueil Malmaison
Technological centre, Wismar

2000 Leone d'Oro at the VII Mostra Internazionale di Architettura in Venice (Venice Biennale)
The Hotel, Lucerne
Agbar Tower, Barcelona
Cultural centre, Lucerne
Science Park, Mons
Palais de Justice, Nantes
Expo 2000, Hannover

2001 Received the Premio Borromini for the project for the cultural centre in Lucerne
The Royal Institute of British Architects awarded him the Gold Medal
13° Praemium Imperial Career Prize in Architecture
Exhibit "Jean Nouvel" at the Centre Georges Pompidou in Paris
Brembo Science Park, Kilometro Rosso, Bergamo
Mutations, Bordeaux
Guthrie Theater, Minneapolis
Council housing, Mulhouse
Installation for the Brazilian exhibit at the Guggenheim Museum in New York
Andel shopping centre, Prague
Gasometer, Vienna

2002 Awarded a *laurea Honoris Causa* by the University of Naples
Awarded an Honorary Doctorate by the Royal College of Art in London
Musée Cité Nature, Arras
Expo 2002, Morat

2003 Awarded an Honorary Doctorate by the Royal Academy of Art in Copenhagen
Hotel Puerta America, Madrid
Les Halles, Paris (competition project)
Ferrari factory, Modena (competition project)
Opera House, Taiching, Taiwan
Railway station, Geneva

2004 Port of Genoa, Genoa
Winery, Aix-en Provence
University complex, Shinjuku-Ku
Federal Polytechnic, Lausanne

2005 Received the Wolf Foundation Prize in Arts
Multi-functional building, Vienna
Port complex, Rabat
Guggenheim Foundation, Guadalajara
Residential complex, Ibiza

2006 Performing Arts Center, Seoul
Building C1, Boulogne-Billancourt

Works

Presentation texts for the sections "The Works" and "The Projects"
are taken from the project reports drawn up by Ateliers Jean Nouvel

Institut du Monde Arabe, Paris

Paris, France, 1981-1987

The building seen from the Seine

The Institute is the showcase of the Arab world in Paris. Thus, it is not an Arab building, but a Western one. Like all cultural centres, it has the function of opening towards all types of people, not just Arabs, and it must be capable of attracting the highest number of visitors possible. Staking everything on attractiveness, it has adopted a Western cultural programme similar to the paradigmatic one of the Beaubourg: the institute houses a museum, temporary exhibits, a library, rooms dedicated to current events, etc., but nothing that is more

particularly specific or sensitive to Arab culture. Forming squares and polygons of greater or lesser size, the *moucharabieh* play on geometry in a way that that recalls the Alhambra.

A second symbolic value that is highlighted is water. Relaxing, it falls from a *shaddar* (a stairway inside the garden on which the glistening water runs), descending from on high, from the sky, along a staircase of about 30 metres.

A true fountain under glass, in which real mercury has been added, preserved from

nitrogen, in remembrance of the interior of the palaces of One Thousand and One Nights. The Institut du Monde Arabe is a building that unites two cultures and two histories.

To the south is modern Paris, with Jussieu; to the north, the historical city with the Ile Saint-Louis and the Ile de la Cité.

If the south façade of the Institute reveals the modernly oriental character of the diaphragms, the north façade stands as a mirror of Western culture.

In effect, the nearest Paris landscape is impressed upon the north façade through a process employing enamel on glass, like an image on its support. This façade, crossed by lines, refers to contemporary art.

In architecture, it is necessary to take a cultural position, to avoid any sort of recipe or pre-packaged solution, and encourage an approach to global and specific problems. For this reason, and with the conviction that the borders between architecture, interior decoration and design are artificial, the project was also concerned with the museum aspect, the design of the exhibitors and the elements of the decor.

The historical centre of Paris seen from the terrace on the top floor of the curvilinear body

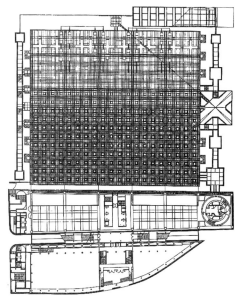

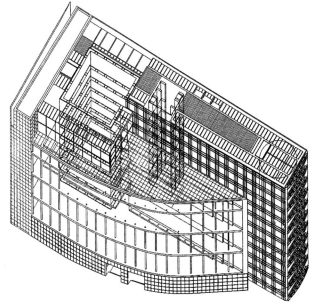

Above
View of the reading room

Right
Plan of the sixth floor

Opposite page
Above
The façade of the building
Below
Plan of the ground floor
and axonometry

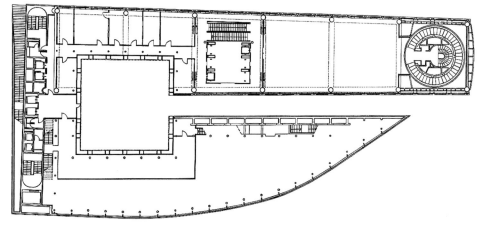

L'Opéra
Lyon, France, 1986-1993

General view

Located in a prestigious position, L'Opéra, a true point of reference for the contemporary, designs the centrality of the Hotel de Ville district, and appears against the sky on the Rhône, in the same way as the glass window of the Grand Palais. It is imposing, simple and monumental: the monumentality of the glass semi-cylinder that doubles the height of the historical building and the simplicity of the homogeneous treatment of the sheets of glass arranged like Venetian blinds that shape the barrel vault. The entrance for the public from the Place de la Comédie is, as in the past, through the colonnade that runs along the

three sides of the building and underlines the urban continuity between the interior and the exterior. Access to the great hall is through opaque revolving doors, brief transitions which, once passed through, lead to the perception, once inside the open volume in the upper part of its thirty metres of height, of the plastic, massive, dark wrapping of the hall. This monumental machine/edifice, totally suspended, pushing away the limits of its supports, seems to levitate.

During the intervals, two foyers welcome the public. In the first, which preserves the original nineteenth century spirit, and which has been subject to a sophisticated job of renovation, a single mirror leads back to and multiplies the lights and the gilding; a second one, placed in the upper part, behind the west spandrel wall, offers a panoramic view of the city. Located under the upper foyer, the restaurant with a terrace enjoys a privileged position, opposite the Hotel de Ville and behind the statues. Like superstructures, against the volume of the stage, the dressing halls of the artists can be glimpses through the glass window. The spaces for the dance company, in the upper part of the building, exploit the entire breadth of the vault. The whole of the building, with the exception of the hall, is treated with sobriety, using

contemporary vocabulary in a register that alternates transparency and opacity. Nouvel wanted the opera house to be like a beating heart. Inside, he wanted to juxtapose two systems; he kept the gilding of the foyer, treating the new surfaces, in polished black granite, like mirrors.

Façade

p. 42
from the top
Plan of the first, third and seventh levels

p. 43
View of the performance hall

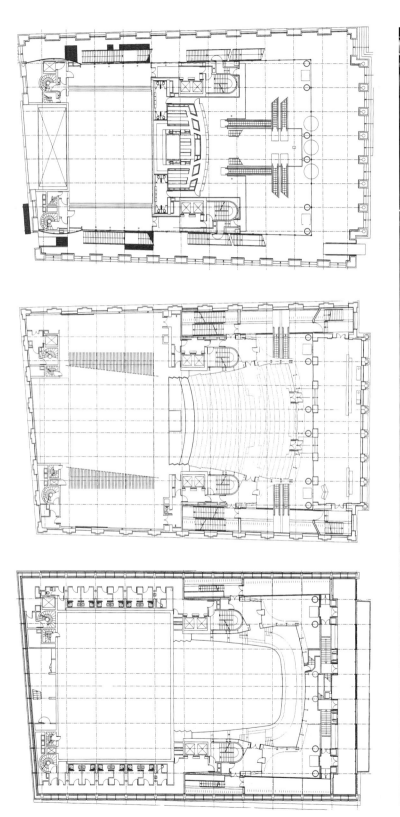

Fondation Cartier
Paris, France, 1991-1994

Sections

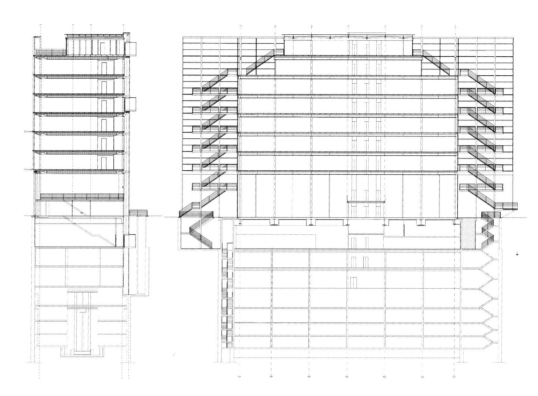

The phantom of the park, in its transparency, to include. The trees show through the high glassed-in enclosure that has taken the place of a long blind wall closed by an eight-metre high wall that they softly brush up against. The Chateaubriand cedar rises solitary, framed by two screens that highlight the entrance. The visitor passes under the cedar and enjoys the spectacle of trees that surround the glassed-in exhibit space, which also – according to a process that interprets the site in depth – rises to a height of 8

metres. In the summer, the great sliding glass walls are opened and the space is transformed into a prolongation of the park articulated by high posts.

This architecture is based on total lightness, and is made of a delicate web of glass and steel. It tends towards the tangible limits of the building and makes the reading of a solid volume superfluous, in the poetics of evanescence. When the virtual challenges reality, architecture must have the courage to take on the image of contradiction.

View of the façade with the main entrance

View of the interior spaces
and the courtyard on the
first floor

Opposite page
Detail of the façade

Palais de Justice
Nantes, France, 1993-2000

The building seen from the Loire

On the nature of justice and its representation in architecture. In official architecture, power must also have its representation. A judicial city is the symbol of the power of justice. To speak of an image of justice makes sense since in terms of symbology, the public building conceals within itself a legacy of signs that cannot be approached without risks. This architecture is the materialization of this legacy, and in it, Nouvel has tried to carefully define

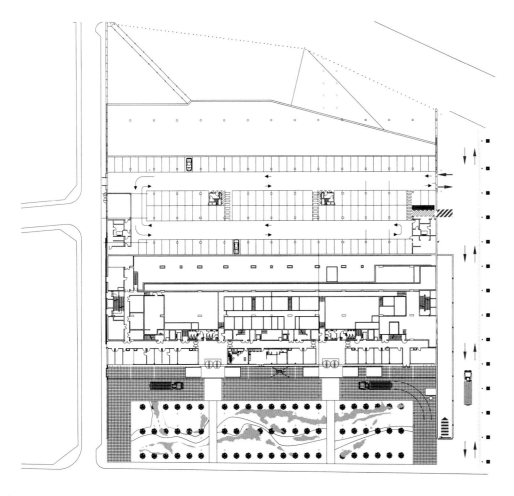

Plan of level 0

p. 50
Above
View of the courtroom
Below
East and north elevation

p. 51
View of the interior

correct architecture. From a distant reading — with the city seen from the other bank — until the detail of the interior spaces, inevitably passing by the façade. A treatise on architectural composition, on objectification.

The passage from the meaning of words to the sign constructed through notions of exactness, justice, equity, balance, dignity, character — the definition of which makes these terms cross other concepts, other ideas.

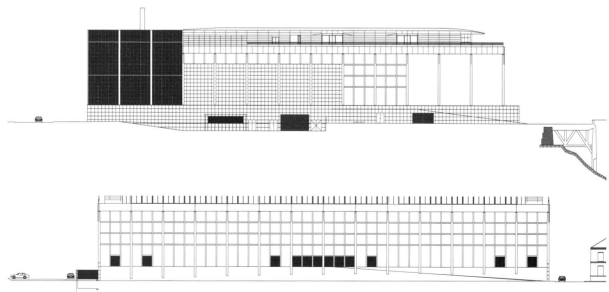

Expansion of the Museo Nacional Centro de Arte Reina Sofia, Madrid

Madrid, Spain, 1999-2005

View of the new inner courtyard

We could define it "in the shadow of Queen Sofia", since the project for the expansion of the museum does not intend to overshadow the previous structure, but rather to enhance it, or illuminate it.

The great, austere construction, "besieged" by its glass elevators and the place where modern and contemporary masterpieces are housed, must impose its force with simplicity and power, and the project must show fidelity, respect and a sense of belonging to and continuity with the past.

The museum expands. Its territory is increased by annexing part of the neighbourhood, but without bashing or traumatizing it – on the contrary, it tries to give it value.

The museum annexes a triangular lot to the west, three or four buildings and a few trees: the buildings are transformed, but stay approximately in the same place, their rapport with the nearby architecture does not change, but the west façade of the museum is set free. The front part of this façade, with its steel facing, is surrounded by glass to protect projectors and screens. This little glass tower completes the family of those that dot the other façades of the museum.

Only two walls are maintained as the symbol of the previous construction, not for their intrinsic beauty, but to underline the change. The trees, too, were kept, and in changing, the three new buildings are organized around a courtyard.

Each of them has a different function: the first, to the south, is a library; the second, to the west, is an auditorium, protocol room, bar and restaurant; the third, to the north, is dedicated to temporary exhibits, and is the only one linked to the original museum.

All three end with terraces that are either public or belong to the offices. The library has variable lighting: from the top, it is

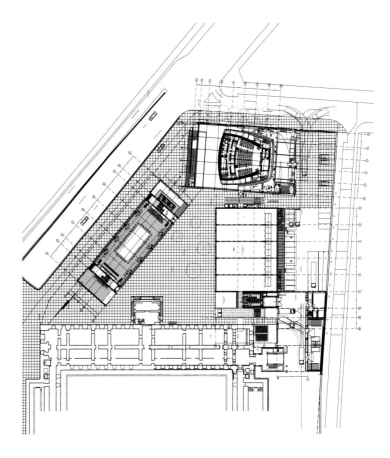

diffused by thick, etched glass cupolas, while great glass walls are darkened by blinds in pierced steel, little refinements that create intimacy and furnish the right intensity for reading. The rooms for temporary exhibits, arranged on three levels, offer many spaces that can be used in different ways.

Planimetry

Above
The exterior of the building that houses the library

Left
The new coffee shop

Opposite page
View of the inner courtyard from above

Agbar Tower
Barcelona, Spain, 1999-2005

The silhouette of the tower seen in the urban context

Not a tower, a skyscraper in the American sense of the word, but a unique object that emerges in the centre of a rather calm city. However, the Agbar Tower is not a slender, nervous vertical line, like an arrow, or like the bell towers that generally punctuate horizontal cities. Instead, it is a fluid mass that perforates the soil, a geyser with permanent, measured-out pressure.

The surface of the building evokes water: smooth, continuous as well as vibrant and transparent, since the material can be read in

depth, colourful and uncertain, luminous and shady. This architecture comes from the earth, but does not have the weight of stone. Even if it were a distant echo of old Catalan formal obsessions carried on the wind the blows in from Monserrat. The irregularity of the material and the light make the bell tower of Agbar vibrate against the skyline of Barcelona. A faraway mirage during the day as well as at night. A sign of entrance into the new diagonal of Plaza de Las Glorias, singular symbol of an international metropolis.

The top of the tower seen from the inside

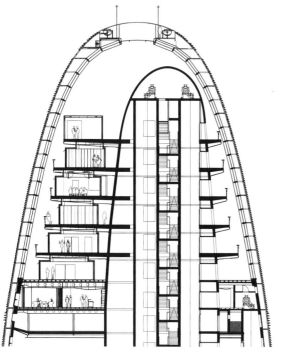

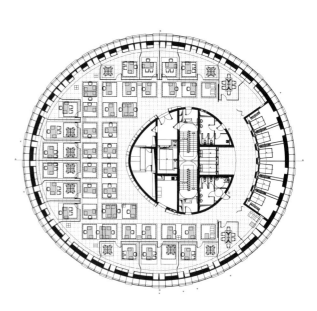

The tower at night

Opposite page
Above
Detail of the ventilated
façade
Below
Section and plan
of a typical floor

Musée du Quai Branly
Paris, France, 1999-2006

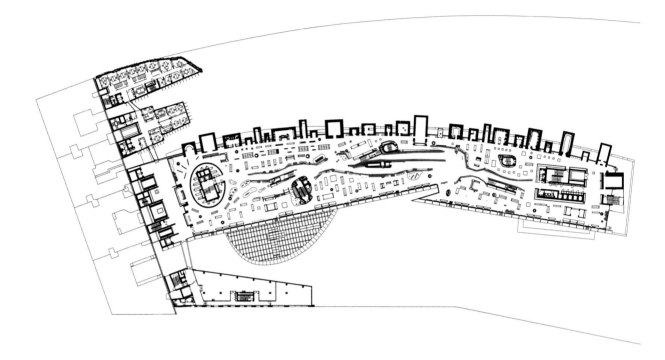

Plan of the first floor

Presence absence, or selective dematerialization. The museum is built around a collection. Here everything is conceived of to arouse participation in the emotion of which the object is the original carrier, but also to protect against light and to capture the few rays of sunlight indispensable to make the space of spirituality vibrate. It is a place marked by the symbols of the forest, of the river, by the obsession with death and oblivion.

It is the place in which censured or denigrated works conceived of in Australia or America find a home. A populated, inhabited space, a space where the ancestral spirits of men engage in dialogue, and men, who discover their human condition, created gods and beliefs. A unique, poetic and unsettling place. The architecture that comes from it has an unexpected nature. Are we before an archaic object? An expression of regression? Far from it.

60

Actually, in order to arrive at this result, the most advanced techniques were used: the glass windows are large, very large, extremely clear, often impressed with immense photographs; the pillars are arranged randomly, and their dimensions could make them appear to be trees or totems; there are photovoltaic cells on the carved or painted wooden sunscreens. However, the means have only relative importance; what counts instead is the result: the raw material seems to disappear at times, one has the impression that the museum is simply a shelter in the woods, without a façade. When the dematerialization encounters the expression of signs, it becomes selective. Here the illusion cradles the work of art. Yet the poetics of the situation still has to be invented, and it is a gentle staggering: the Parisian garden becomes sacred wood, and in its depths, the museum dissolves.

The north façade with its "vegetal wall" created by Patrick Blanc

p. 62
Above
Detail of the north façade
Below
Longitudinal section

p. 63
Above
View of the great exhibit gallery
Below
Cross section

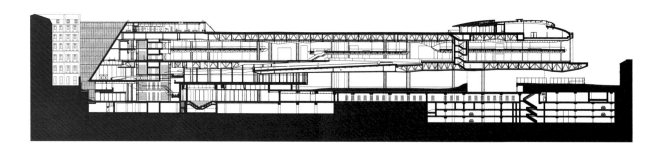

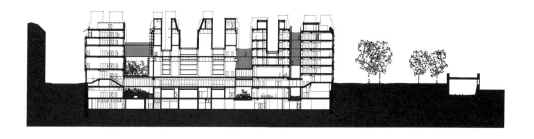

Guthrie Theater

Minneapolis, Minnesota, Usa, 2001-2007

General view

Opposite page
Plan of the first floor

p. 66
Above
Façade facing the river
Below
Cross section

p. 67
View of the performance
hall

Located on the point in which the orthogonal scheme of the city encounters the spectacular landscape of the Mississippi, the new Guthrie Theater welcomes and reconciles the typical elements of the urban context of Minneapolis. The building relates to the heights of the two towers of the downtown area as it relates to the metallic cylinders of the silos, to then go beyond the water and enter the domain of the river, where industrial activities take place. In this project, the past and the contemporary are reconciled, and the Guthrie, in the midst of mills and suspended walkways, comes forward with legitimate ambition to become a historical symbol projected towards the future: the new industry of vital, creative theatre culture in Minneapolis. To evoke the chimney of a factory, in fact, is the sleek body of the sign that, spreading messages by means of its leds, functions as a signal to announce initiatives and performances on the skyline. Inside, the Guthrie Theater has three rooms linked by a transversal pathway: the semi-cylindrical volume of the Trust Stage, with 1,100 seats; the rectangular one of the frontal room, with 700; and finally an experimental room with 250 seats, with a foyer and orange *boite* illuminated at night. These volumes are expertly combined through vertical superimposition, creating great empty spaces of distribution from which to observe the breathtaking view of the city. The balance between performance and intermission, between time for theatre and time for socialization, between representation and interrelation is the guiding theme of the project, with the aim of making an evening spent in the theatre a time for rejoicing and communality.

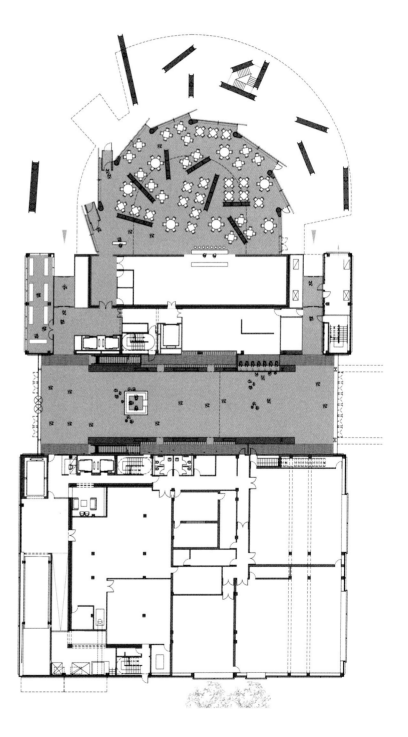

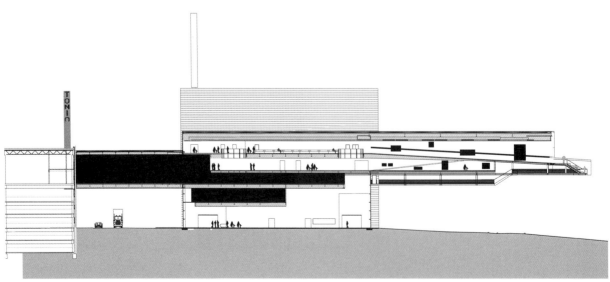

Brembo Science Park, Kilometro Rosso
Bergamo, Italy, 2004-2007

View of the façade towards
the motorway

Opposite page
General planimetry, design
of the project

*Project for the interiors of the
Centro Ricerche e Sviluppo di
Brembo:* Blast Architetti -
Bombassei, Siccardi, Traversa

The project for the Parco Scientifico
Tecnologico di Brembo involves an area near
Bergamo, along the A4 Milano-Venezia
motorway. Jean Nouvel can take the credit for
the master plan of the Kilometro Rosso
research park and the Brembo centre for
research and development.
The Brembo project calls for the creation of
offices, laboratories for design and for the
development of prototypes for high-

technology brakes. The Kilometro Rosso is a
red wall, conceived of to separate an artificial
area, the motorway and the red outdoor
parking area, from a green, natural area, a
landscaped garden where the glass buildings
that house the offices and research
laboratories have been located. The wall is
supported by a structure in reinforced
concrete and steel completely covered with a
facing of interlocking red extruded aluminium

profiles. The morphology and width of the wall in correspondence to the Brembo research and development area are transformed to host the scenographic horizontal pathways of the new building.

The Brembo complex was conceived of to host two different structural types: the lower parts of the buildings, including the underground part, are in reinforced concrete, while the structure of the upper parts is in steel. The protruding parts of the building are supported by vierendel beams, and all of the flooring, in pre-compressed concrete floorboards, collaborates with the structure.

The Kilometro Rosso has a steel structure that supports the outer wrapping through an extruded aluminium profile on one side and the inner shell in prefabricated panels on the other. The curved façade is the result of the curvature of the main structure, with geometry that varies in section every 3 metres.

The outdoor parking area is in bright red epoxy resin. The outer wrapping of the wall is in extruded aluminium profiles, protected by dazzling red shellac. The criterium underlying the Brembo project can be defined according to a "shell and nucleus" structure.

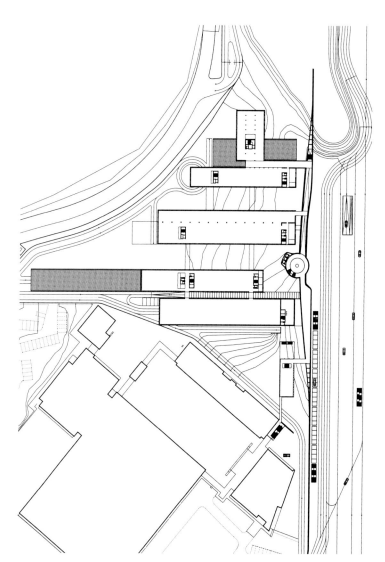

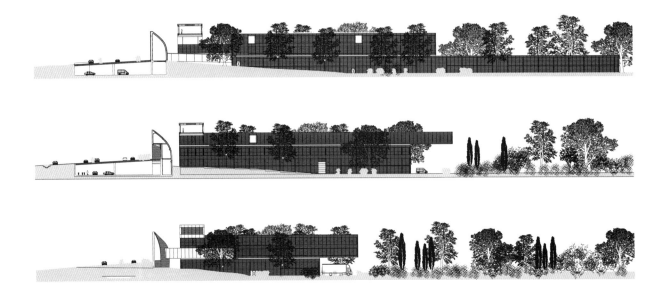

Above
Elevations

Below
Detail of the entrance

Opposite page
Detail of the façade

Projects

Concert House Danish Radio
Copenhagen, Denmark, 2002 (under construction)

Below
Elevations

Opposite page
Above
Rendering of the wrapping
of the concert hall
Below
View of the concert hall

Building in a new neighbourhood is a risky mission. You can only respond to an uncertain future with the positive force of uncertainty: mystery – mystery that is never separated from seduction, and hence from attraction. It is necessary to evaluate the context, whatever it might be. In order to reach this goal, it is necessary to establish a presence, an identity. The proposal is thus to materialize the territory by creating exceptional urban equipment that respects the planned urban geometry. This will be a volume that will let its interiority be guessed at, a mysterious parallelepiped that is capable of changing according to the variation of the light during the day or at night. At night the volume will become a theatre of images, of colours of light, showing its intense inner life. The interior is a world of its own, complex and diversified. A street lined with shops follows the urban canal and is invaded by a bar and restaurant. A covered plaza dominates it, a great empty volume underlying the wooden "scales" of the concert hall.

Office Tower
Dhoa, Qatar, 2002 (under construction)

The development of Qatar has started off on a new course aimed at valorising culture and making the nation – and the city of Doha in particular – the cultural pole of the Gulf region. This programme intends to reconfigure the bay of Doha through a landscaping plan of the Corniche and projects for a series of buildings destined to become symbols of the entire coast. Situated between the centre of the city and the Corniche, the tower will occupy a fundamental place in the new landscape. The Doha tower is cylindrical, with a diameter of about 45 metres. It is covered with a vault and ends in an antenna at 231.5 metres from the ground. The structure in steel and cement on a rhomboidal grid bends on the virtual surface of the cylinder. The façade uses a double cladding system. Each floor features a different panoramic view: onto the gulf to the east, onto the port to the south, onto the city to the west and onto the coast and desert to the north. With its tall, slender, glimmering silvery-laced silhouette, the tower is destined to become the symbol of the Corniche and the whole of the city of Doha.

Left
View of the whole tower

Opposite page
Detail of the cladding
of the façade

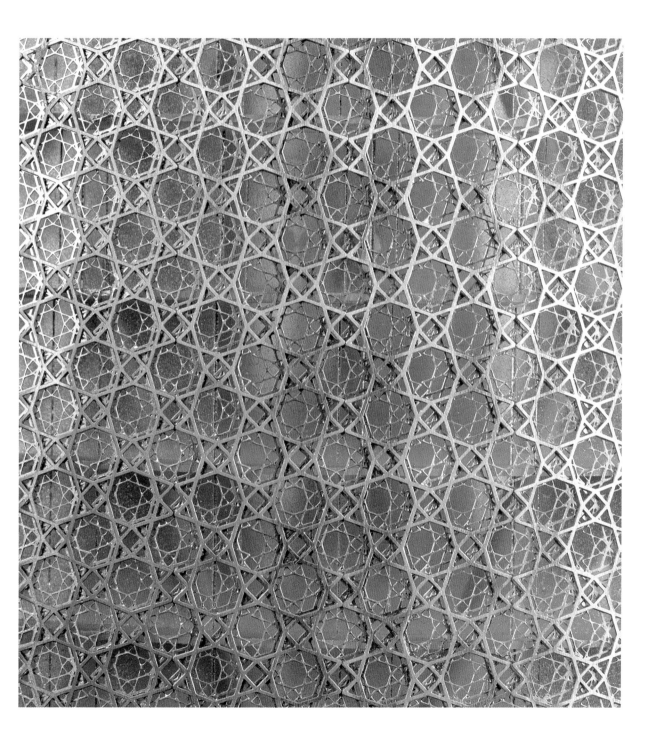

Guggenheim Foundation
Guadalajara, Mexico, 2005 (not carried out)

Below and opposite page
Rendering

In Guadalajara, houses are low and trees are tall. The site where the Omnilife offices rise is near a nature sanctuary. The concept calls for elongating the park in order to give the illusion that the project belongs to that geography, atomising the building into smaller parts in conformity to the scale of the horizontally-oriented development of the city. To work in the garden, to take a stroll under an artificial blue sky that acts as protection from the natural one by making its presence come through, to take a walk under the creeping plants that adorn the metallic grilles that project geometric shadows softened by the rustling of the leaves. And since Guadalajara is the city of Luis Barragan, since colour is a centuries-old tradition, the buildings are colourful — offices of iridescent, changing colours, of red and yellow, or brown and blue — in order to create, under the shadows, an ever new play on the alternation of light and colour.

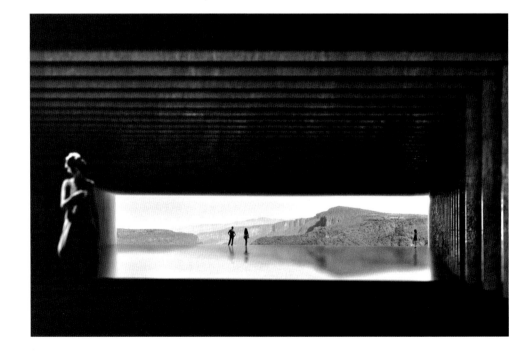

Performing Arts Center

Seoul, Korea, 2006 (contest, winning project)

Korea and Seoul welcome universal music.
Nouvel thought that it would be a positive
idea to place the new opera house in the
centre of the river in order to make nature
and music meet.

The image of Korea has always been
connected with nature: to rocks, to trees, to
the horizon of the sky and to water. It was
the designer's intention that the opera house
become the emblem of all of Korea within
the city of Seuol, on the condition that its
history could be linked to its history and its
essence could be linked with music.

The project originally called for the creation
of a sort of Parisian Ile de la Cité. Later it
was decided to build – rather than an island
of the city, an island *in* the city, an artificial
element that would be located in the centre
of the modern metropolis together with
natural elements: mountains, rocks, trees,
thus becoming the symbol of the landscape
and the Korean soul. This reflection gave
birth to the proposal of creating an island of

music, using a very mysterious type of
architecture. And at night, illuminated by
reflectors, architecture could evoke the
reality of dream.

La Philharmonie
Paris, France, 2007 (contest, winning project)

Opposite page
Rendering, opposite view
of the exterior and of the
performance hall

La Philharmonie exists as a prestigious occurrence in harmonious relation to the Parc de la Villette, la Cité de la Musique and the Boulevard Périphérique.
First: in harmony with the light of Paris.
Second: in harmony with the Parc de la Villette.
Third: in harmony with the Cité de la Musique
Fourth: in harmony with the suburban Boulevard and the banlieu.
La Philharmonie is an open place.
First: the hall and the foyer are pleasant places where you can make a date, spend time looking at the shops, eating or drinking in the bistrots with a view onto the garden, read in the reading rooms.
Second: the performance hall, which evokes immaterial bands of music and light, suspends the audience-listeners in space, on long balconies.
Third: it is a question of giving lustre back to the concert, to this unique experience that is not exclusively represented by the rapture of the music, but also by the visual and sensorial involvement, by creating pleasure, that desire that accompanies the most prestigious philharmonic halls, and the one in Paris must also become part of.

Louvre Abu Dhabi
Abu Dhabi, Qatar, 2007 (studies in progress)

Opposite page
Above
Rendering, view from
the sea
Below
View of the complex under
the double cupola

The museum and the sea. Every climate loves exceptions: warmer when it is cool, cooler when below the tropics. Human beings, like works of art, suffer from thermal shock. The project of the Louvre in Abu Dhabi has been influenced by ascertainments that are just as elementary. It wants to create a welcoming world that takes in light and shadow in serenity, reflecting them and placating them. It wants to belong to a country, to its history and its geography without being a dull translation, a neoplasm that means boredom and conventionality. It would like to emphasize the fascination of rare encounters. It is unusual to find a constructed archipelago in the sea, and it is even a less frequent occurrence that it might be protected by an umbrella that creates showers of light.

It is not clear how one might come up alongside it in a boat, find piers to for access on foot from the coast, or how guests might be received to visit the unique collections, to linger in the tempting bookstores or taste tea, coffee and the flavours of local gastronomy. It is a calm, complex place. A contrast between a series of museums that cultivate their differences and their authenticity.

It is a project based on one of the main signs of Arab architecture, the cupola, which is here interpreted in a modern key through the gap it establishes with tradition. The double cupola is flat, 180 metres in diameter, with perfect radiating geometry, perforated like an irregular piece of cloth in order to obtain shadow punctuated by light. The cupola is resplendent in the Abu Dhabi sun. At night, this sheltered landscape becomes an oasis of light under a starry sky. The Abu Dhabi Louvre thus becomes the culmination of an urban course. Garden on the coast, oasis of freshness, luminous shelter day and night, its aesthetics reveals how it is in accordance with its function of sanctuary of very precious works of art.

Tour Signal
La Défense, Paris, 2008 (under construction)

In July 2007, EPAD (Etablissement Public d'Aménagement de La Défense) launched an appeal for the construction of a tower capable of giving new energy to the image of the prime European business district. For the fiftieth anniversary of La Défense, the promoters hoped in effect to "make a major architectural gesture to the world, a gesture bearing creative vigour, formal audacity and technological modernity".

Thus at the gates of Paris, west of the Grande Arche, the tower conceived of by Jean Nouvel rises. The architect, who chose the site to open La Défense to Puteaux in the western suburbs, had the aim of creating a strong polarity in the heart of the Ile-de-France, while drawing the project in to relation with its constructed and natural environment.

Chosen from among eighteen candidatures, of which five were retained for the competition, Jean Nouvel's project expresses a new type of "mixed" building, which allows a multitude of activities to co-exist inside the same building: 140,000 square metres are thus occupied by collective spaces (offices, hotels, shops, restaurants and publics and cultural amenities) and housing. This functional combination was one of the constraints written in the specifications, as was environmental quality (innovative solutions permitting significant use of renewable sources of energy) and respect for the rules of durable development. The problem of the quality of life and of well-being is equally expressed in the project through the new concept of Very High Emotional Quality (Très Haute Qualité Emotionnelle).

With its 301 metres and sixty-one floors, the building will be the highest in France. It is characterized by four stacked blocks, each including an atrium forming a huge window on one of the four sides. It is a regular, rectangular shape; its style, classic. The tower, which will employ many luminous effects, will present on each of its sides, on the level of the atriums, an immense screen of animated colour. Its delivery is set for 2015.

The powerful silhouette of the Signal will make it possible to re-establish the balance of the landscape all around the Grande Arche.

Thought

Louisiana Manifesto*

In 2005, more than ever, architecture is annihilating places, banalizing them, violating them. Sometimes it replaces the landscape, creates it in its own image, which is nothing but another way of effacing it.

And then there is Louisiana, an emotional shock. The living proof of a forgotten truth: architecture has the power to transcend.

It can reveal geographies, histories, colours, vegetations, horizons, qualities of light.

Impertinent and natural, it is in the world. It lives. It is unique. It is Louisianan.

It is a microcosm, a bubble. No image, no statement can plumb its depth. You have to be there to experience it, to believe it.

It is an expansion of our world at a time when that world is getting smaller.

[...]

We must establish sensitive, poetic rules, approaches that will speak of colours, essences, characters, the anomalies of the act of creation, the specificities of rain, wind, sea and mountain. Rules that speak of the temporal and spatial continuum, that will turn the tide towards a mutation, a modification of the inherited chaos, and take account of all the fractal scales of our cities.

[...]

By contrast, the ideology of the specific aspires to autonomy, to the use of the resources of the place and the time, to the privileging of the non-material.

How can we use what is here and nowhere else?

How can we differentiate without caricaturing?

How can we achieve depth?

Architectural design on the large scale does not mean inventing ex nihilo.

Architecture means transformation, organizing the mutations of what is already there.

Architecture means encouraging the embedding in the landscape of places that anyway have a tendency to invent themselves. It means to reveal, to give direction.

It means prolonging lived history and its traces of past lives.

It means listening to the breathing of a living place, to its pulsations.

It means interpreting its rhythms in order to create. Architecture should be seen as the modification of a physical, atomic, biological continuum.

As the modification of a fragment situated at the heart of our immense universe amidst the dizzying discoveries made by macro and nanophysics. Whatever the scale of the transformation, of a site or of a place, how are we to communicate the unpredictability of the mutation of a living fragment?

Can we domesticate the visible components — clouds, plant-life, living organisms of every size — with signs, reflections, new plantings?

How does one create a vibration that evokes a hidden depth, a soul?

This is surely a task for poetry, since only poetry can produce "the metaphysics of the instant".

To work at the limits of the achievable - with the mysterious, the fragile, the natural.

To anticipate the weathering of time, patina, materials that change, that age with character.

To work with imperfection as a revelation of the limits of the accessible.

[...]

The detail — like the totality — is an opportunity to invent, to dislocate, to enrich the world, to recompose, to reassemble, to provoke confrontations of textures, lights, of unlikely techniques.

[...]

An architecture that creates singularity in duality, that invents it in the confrontation with a situation, is Louisianan.

[...]

Architecture means the adaptation of the condition of a place to a given time by the willpower, desire and knowledge of certain human beings.

We never do this alone.

We always do it somewhere — certainly for some person or persons, but always also for everyone.

It is time we stopped limiting architecture to the appropriation of a style.

The age needs architects who doubt, who seek without thinking they have found, who put themselves at risk, who rediscover the values of empiricism, who invent architecture as they design it, who surprise themselves, who notice the mildew

* In June 2005, Jean Nouvel was invited to exhibit his works at the Louisiana Museum of Modern Art, near Copenhagen. On that occasion he drew up a manifesto that expressed his ideas on architecture: an appeal to prefer the specific to the generic, the here and now, the present and life, with respect to everywhere and nowhere.

Agbar Tower, interior

on their windows and know how to interpret it. Let's leave the cosmetics of vain cities to the architects who think of themselves as aesthetes. *From now on, let architecture rediscover its aura in the inexpressible, in the cloudy. In the imperfection of what is invented!* The architect is not aware of having come to the end of his work until he slips and slides from creation to modification, from assertion to allusion, from building-up to filling-in, from construction to infiltration, from imposition to superimposition, from the neat to the nebulous, from addition to deviation, from calligraphy to etching, to erasure... Instead of the archaic architectural goal of domination, of making a permanent mark, today we should prefer to seek the pleasure of living somewhere.

Let us remember that architecture can also be an instrument of oppression, a tool for conditioning behaviour.

Let us never permit anyone to censure this pursuit of pleasure, especially in the domain of the familiar and intimate that is so necessary to our wellbeing.

Let us identify ourselves.

Everyone bears a potential world within himself or herself.

Let us be aware of our potential, which is equal to that of any human being – largely unexplored – often poetic, therefore disquieting.

[...]

We want to be able to keep on travelling, to listen to spontaneous music, to live in landscapes as inhabited as a personality, to meet men and women who invent their own culture, to discover unknown colours.

Architecture is the vehicle for variations.

A permanence changed by life and events.

[...]

Architecture has to be impregnated and to impregnate, to be impressionable and impress to absorb and emit.

Let us love architecture that knows how to navigate, that shines like a light, that can let you read the topography, the lie of the land, feel the wind, the skies, the soils, the waters, the fires, the smells, the trees, the grass, the flowers, the mosses... that remembers the usages and customs of the place and at the same time interfaces with the information terminals of our world, that shows us the ages and those who have journeyed through them.

Such architecture is built up in harmony with its time. The stragglers who are still constructing the archetypes of the 20th century are diachronically ill, refusing to live their lives.

Architecture dates. We know it to be mortal, imperilled, as sure as we know it is alive.

And so we watch it emerging from the darkness and imagine that it will return there one day.

The architectures of situation, of the specific, the Louisianan architectures weave this bond between past and future, mineral and vegetal, between the instant and eternity, the visible and the invisible. They are the *genius loci* of emergence and of disappearance. They distill the essence of their own slow, poignant ruin.

This consciousness of time overlays the surprises of the new lives lived in the place, the great rhythms of dawn and twilight the indifference of the inevitable hours of idleness and decay...

Louisianan architectures are dreamed architectures, full of silences, places of forgetfulness but also of archaeology. They become the cue for reinterpretations of an ambivalent past.

Louisianan architectures move us because they have been dreamed into life, into insecurity, into resistance, sometimes into despair; ruined or assassinated, but never forgotten, because like the Phoenix disappearing in the flames only to be reborn, they make us dream of eternally recurring points of light...

The uncertainty, the simplicity and even the modesty of the Louisianan materials and resources hold out the hope that Louisianan architecture can continue to exist in any economic conditions.

That it can filter through even to the shameful shantytowns of our global politics...

And to see the beauty in the precariousness of poverty is not to forget the desperate conditions. It is simply to see the power and dignity of life in extreme situations and to experience the unplumbed depths of humanity to be found there.

[...]

Exploration is a duty, understanding is an intense desire, questioning is a condition of evolution.

We think with our senses, we feel with our thoughts.

Contradictions generate sparks.

Sensations generate emotions.

Emotions generate love, love the desire to live, to share, to give, to extend our life into others.

Architecture is connecting, belonging, interfering, it is yea-saying and nay-saying.

But it is also harmonizing the inanimate with the living.

Harmony is not always soothing; it can be a source of unimaginable pleasure, of a hope beyond hope, an elevation of our imaginative powers.
Pleasure is sometimes the improbable but indispensable catalyst that transforms intelligent doubt or honest despair into a conquering force.
[...]
Architecture is a gift from the deepest part of yourself.
It is the making of worlds, the invention of places, of micropleasures, microsensations, quick dips into reality.
Let architecture be vibrant, perpetually echoing the changing universe!
Let it build temporary oases for nomads in search of the directions, the desires that form them as long as they live!
How can we mark out, how can we fence in our lifespan?
How can we petrify serenity, calm, delight, far less ecstasy, intoxication, euphoria, jubilation?
[...]
Chance brings us encounters to be exploited, situations to be invented!

This arid architecture should be used as a support, a point of departure for odd, dislocated, exploded, inverted strategies.
One of the missions of Louisianan architecture is to complete, to re-orient, to diversify, to modify and to imagine what the generic architectures can never imagine: the lifetimes to which they will give shelter.
Let us be Louisianans! Let us resist!
Let us reclaim the architectures of the improbable!
Those that unite praxis and poetry to leave their imprint on a place, to throw in their lot with that place.
Let us be Louisianans in all these territories: from Petra to Sanaa, from Venice to Manhattan, from Chartres to Ronchamp, from fishermen's huts to the tents of the desert, from the favelas of Rio to the industrial ruins of the Ruhr, from Katsura to Louisiana…
All clashes of temporalities and illuminations, all poetic paradoxes.
The miraculous paradoxes that Paul Valéry summed up in this simple line: *"Time scintillates and dream is knowledge"*.

Hisao Suzuki

Institut du Monde Arabe, Paris 1993
p. 94

Philippe Ruault

Hotel, Lucerne 2000
pp. 96, 97

Hotel Puerta America, Madrid 2005
pp. 98-99

Gasometer, Vienna 2001
pp. 100, 101

Guthrie Theater, Minneapolis 2006
pp. 102, 103

Palais de Justice, Nantes 2000
pp. 104, 105

Musée du Quai Branly, Paris 2006
pp. 106, 107

Georges Fessy

Institut du Monde Arabe, Paris 1987, 2000
pp. 108, 109

Photographers

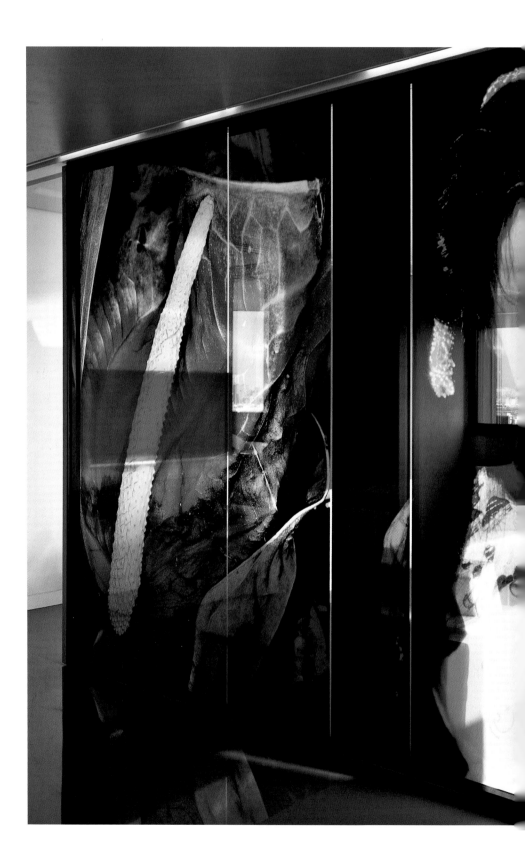

Critique

The Thought of a Creator of Images

Olivier Boissière
Jean Nouvel

Jean Nouvel is not a saint. Coming to the capital from his southwest more like Cyrano than Rastignac, he was trained in the diatribe with noisy masters like Claude Parent and Paul Virilio, before discovering, in the tumult of May '68 and in those exercises of direct democracy, an unexpected talent of enthusiastic tribune (and stuttering for a long time!). His physique and air of an important actor have made him – and he has by no means put up any resistance – the darling of the press, to the shame of his confrères. He gives lectures, travels around the planet, answers every question as if, as Starck rightly underlines, he has the obligation of expressing himself when he is given the floor. He could end up being a celebrity because of his fame. But, as his friend and colleague Paul Gehry says, "To be noticed isn't everything". It would truly be nothing if Nouvel did not, building after building, give proof of it through the "constructed" of his know-how (art is doing or making).

From the time he founded his first firm in 1970 – even before he took his degree – the life of the architect Jean Nouvel developed on various fronts. First of all, he built: it is in the construction yard that you see the architect. From the time of his first work for Claude Parent, when he was barely twenty-one, and as he himself confessed, totally ignorant of the art of building, until his first important creations at the end of the decade, Nouvel best exploited the few possibilities that were offered to beginners: homes for acquaintances, a small experimental school, remodelling jobs, expanding buildings – the daily bread of an apprentice. He was an activist with his young colleagues, and founded a rebel movement and a union that was opposed to the near-sighted corporativism of the Order of Architects, guardian of the *status quo*. He was one of the active organizers of the counter-competition for Les Halles, a flash of pride that brought together the best of the international intelligentsia: Roland Barthes and Henri Lefèbvre, Philip Johnson and Tomás Maldonado. He organized the Paris

Biennials of young artists under the auspices of the critic Georges Boudaille. He took part in competitions on the spur of the moment, the only way to get commissions. He studied theatre projects, the prelude to the construction of the theater in Belfort. From these confused experiences, the architect gradually drew up not a sketched out theory, but a series of precepts. He faced fields and problems that served as a pretext for the definition and elaboration of a correct attitude. The habit of working beside future users enabled him to set precise limits: if everything that concerned the programme implied democratic (or political) responsibility, cultural responsibility – giving form – is the responsibility of the architect.

The study of previous theatrical projects gave him a clear idea of the attitude to adopt towards history: juxtaposition – and, that is, without clashing – of the ancient and the modern, accentuation of their characteristics without pastiches, without imitations (but perhaps ambiguity). His colleague Jacques Le Marquet suggested that the stage set was not just a matter of the stage: Nouvel's architecture would be intense and sensational, spectacular in a positive way. From his period as an activist, he kept a burning desire to convince (and diffidence towards politicians) and the taste for critical architecture. Familiarity with artistic matters enabled him to measure the wealth of a substratum that was incomparable for the architect.

Around the end of the 1970s, Nouvel had already planned different constructions that attracted attention and were at times accused of eclecticism. In his haste and desire to explore all of the possibilities offered to him, he was still only defined in negative terms: listing them helter-skelter, he is not, he will not be, a copier, a *Versaillais*, a repetitive rationalist, a "neu Corbu", an involuntary suprematist, a *banlieue* regionalist… At the time, he willingly stood under the flag of the post-modern, eclectic radicals, makers of "geese" or "decorated hangars", symbolists, the ugly and ordinary, the spectacular, the ironic, all of those who live and translate their season.

1981 marked a turning point in French architecture. New managers had big plans. Even the Prime Minister, François Mitterand, did not hide his ambitions in this field. Nouvel was among the most promising architects of the new generation. He won the first competition of the septennate, the one for the institute of the Arab world. Then he got in on all of the big projects: La Villette and the Ministry of Finance, Tête Défense and the Universal Expo of 1989, the *salle de rock* of Bagnolet and the international conference centre… Without success. He was considered close to power, and would become the architect of the regime: his important creations, a part from IMA and INIST in Nancy, were in Lyon, Tours Dax, Nîmes, under the aegis of more conservative builders on paper, but they were also perhaps better advised and would support him passionately. The mysteries of public matters…
For the entire decade Nouvel was engaged in intense activity: fifteen projects in 1985, another fifteen in 1986, twenty-four in 1987, eighteen in 1988, thirty-six in 1989…
The fame of IMA brought a great deal of commissions.
In the euphoria of the moment, Nouvel only thought of times of scarcity. He pretended to ignore improbable clients, projects without financing, the role of support that he often had to play, the pointless commotion that surrounded him. He became a personality in Paris, and a night owl, too. With the growth of the firm, he decided to choose a new partner, Emmanuel Cattani. He broke with his young partners. Jean-Marc Ibos and Myrto Vitart slammed the door in his face. Emmanuel Blamont was seduced by Brazil and went abroad. An era ended.
At the beginning of the 1980s, Nouvel had laid the tracks of a route that rested on two convictions: architecture cannot put itself forward as an autonomous discipline, closed in itself and oblivious to the world around it; the project, by nature – location, climate, relief, destination, economy, culture – can only be specific. "I will do the same project twice when I am asked the same question twice", he said. What came out of it was a process of elaboration that of necessity implied a rigorous and subtle analysis of all of the elements, the fixation of rules of formation, tests of transferral and of the factors pre-eminent in Foucault's thought – discontinuity, specificity, exteriority, upheaval – and finally, the definition of a concept comprised of a whole of ideas gone through with a fine-tooth comb and governing each and every little detail. A deductive method, the opposite of the Beaux-Arts' method that from a preliminary (and ingenious) idea made the entire musical score come down. In short, a method that would only put forward effective functionalism in a more sophisticated version, if architecture would not have to interrogate the world, give it a meaning. Nouvel's evolution has also gone in that direction: it is absolutely modern. The galaxy of images that he surrounded himself with did not aim at founding a style – that would have contradicted the specific nature of the project – but an aesthetic. It included all of the icons of the present: images of progress and industry, of space and space capsules, of transportation – the belly of the Concorde and the aileron of the F1 – of electronics and its sparkling filaments, and of fiction, the cinema, advertising and show business. Nouvel's aesthetic is inclusive: it contrasts genres and sensations, hard and soft, smooth and rough, the show of technology and its rusty degradation. This vision full of contrasts has its origins in contemporary art: Nouvel expressed his preference for the artists Joseph Beuys and Walter De Maria, Donald Judd, Robert Smithson and Richard Serra and Dan Flavin. He came across influences, extending them to the landscape. He considered with equal attention the "works" of land art and man's signs on the territory, motorways with guard-rails, escarpments, tollbooths, ports with cranes, drawbridges, dense accumulations of garishly coloured containers, airports with their immense hangars, grass beaten down by the whir of reactors and pointillist illumination. It is a dynamic vision: speed and displacement find a natural place. It is here that Nouvel finds the equivalent of his vision in that of the cineaste: panning. Zoom, frame, field and counter-field, the shot from above and below are inscribed on his

buildings like architectural elements, in an explicit collusion with the modern gaze, lucid and tender, that scrutinizes the jungle of the city, abandoned lands, the vacuity under the motorways, parking lots like those of his friend from Berlin Wim Wenders. Against the proper, expert and magnificent play of volumes in the light, Nouvel fights for architecture that produces images. The competition for the Tour sans fins, won in 1989 by Nouvel and by his future ex-partner Ibos, marked a decisive step in his career, propelling him forward into the cosmopolitan club of architects in the limelight. The benefits of his new collaboration with Emmanuel Cattani were not mingy: modernization and computerization of the firm, widening of the field. Projects abroad came in profusion – in the Low Countries and in Germany, Switzerland and Austria, with sporadic excursions in the Far East and Australia… During this productive period, Nouvel did not change his "young architect" attitude: he took part in big contests, won very few, took the risk of invention and paid the price. The most bitter example is the Grand Stade of Saint-Denis. The risks of uncontrolled growth took him to the brink of disaster: he was saved only by a handful of faithful friends.

During this period Nouvel added a few entries to his prize-list: the black, red and gold of the Opéra in Lyon, the discreet UFO of the Conference Centre in Tours, the glimmering colours of the triangle of the station in Lille. And another building "never seen before", the Cartier in Paris, a splendid way to thumb his nose at all defamers of transparency. Transparency, or rather "trans-appearance", as previously affirmed, was certainly one of his primary obsessions, one of his newest and most stubbornly held convictions. It goes back to the project for the DDE in Poitiers, in 1979. It later passed through all of the phases, from more or less total inclusion – the first Cartier property in Jouy-en-Josas – to the pure isolated object like the Tête Défense (but can one isolate the sky from the horizon?). Play on depth of field was enriched, on the superimposition of textures and filters, of which IMA is a singular example. He plays with nature and the landscape to include them and/or frame them as he likes. He places space and form in an abyss with a simple play of light and matter. Nouvel's buildings tend to cancel out the weight of matter, to make it impalpable. The Cartier building and the construction in Friedrichstrasse in Berlin push architecture towards hitherto unknown limits. But the search for virgin territory is Nouvel's insurpressable vocation.

Then others enter – the sharecroppers, to reap and sow. The conquerors are already elsewhere, and this is annoying to many. For that matter, France does not lend an ear to its most audacious conquistadors of space. Nations and institutions prefer more domestic heroes. They do not worry about their conquistadors: and so they always go back to sea.

O. Boissière, *Jean Nouvel*, Rusconi Libri per Idea Libri, Santarcangelo di Romagna 2003, pp. 9-16. Italian edition ed. Artemisia progetti editoriali, Genoa, translated by Mario Barboni. Original ed., O. Boissière, *Jean Nouvel*, Pierre Terrail Edition, Paris 1999. Published with permission of Vilo Group.

Alejandro Zaera
Strategies of desire: production of affects

The greater the complexity of a system, its dependence on external forces, the greater the need for strategy as an operative mode. Strategic operativity is contingent on possible decisions of others, who are in turn contingent on our actions; an operativity without start or end, instantaneous. Nouvel works firstly through the suspension of aesthetic judgment. *As in rap*, instrumental technique is devalued by expressive forms with a much higher integrating capacity[1]. Mixing board techniques, *sampling and scratching*: they not only allow the literal inclusion of multiple segments of reality in the musical construction, but they make disciplinary virtuosism inoperative. Like most contemporary creators of any interest, Nouvel moves away from ideals of *modernity* and the *Enlightenment project* in their precepts of *rationalization*, *secularization* and *differentiation* that had come to replace the traditional religious vision.

He dismantles its organic unit into independent domains: science, art and morality, each one mastered by its own internal logic.

Nouvel's pragmatic aesthetics eliminates these boundaries, collapses the aesthetic *distancement* that permitted the humanistic construction of an active subjectivity and a passive objectivity. Avoid the estranged, critical experience: as in pornography and *rap*, the object annuls the power of the perceptive ego through the production of a relationship of *fascination*.[2]

A strategy that was inaugurated by Duchamp and that is often used as an art technique, for example by Jeff Koons.

Nouvel proposes a strategy of situations; with the scenographer Jacques Le Marquet, he develops an operative mode based on the construction of *situations* instead of topographic or geometric models. A strategy to exploit desire as a *mediation* between *subject* and *object*: what the situationists would call to eliminate "artificially generated distances"[3].

Nouvel explores the dense materiality of desire through the intensification of dubious pleasures: to

Expansion of the Museo
Nacional Centro de Arte
Reina Sofía, Madrid

find delight in reproducing the most banal scenographies of consumer society, coating a cultural centre with the skin of a supermarket, designing the highest tower of Europe, dressing a rock venue in *heavy metal* icons, …using the cheapest tricks: catwalks, paints and screens, vertigo and bedazziement, violent ompressions and expansions.

…Strategies with neither depth nor rhetoric, that offer no social redemption. It is not an *aesthetics of disappearance* but rather of *intensification*; it works trough a productive intensification of the real, rather through a simulated aesthetics, a nostalgia of reality.

[1] See the analysis of *rap* techniques and ideologies as a prototype form of creation of a pragmatic aesthetics. "*The Fine Art of Rap*", Richard Schusterman. *Pragmatist Aesthetics: Living Beauty. Rethinking Art.* Cambridge, Mass: Blackwell Publishers, 1992.

[2] "What happens when you see, even from a distance, seems to touch you with a grasping contact, when seeing becomes contact at a distance? What happens when what you see is imposed on your gaze, as if the gaze were touched, captured, put in touch with appearance?" Maurice Blachot, *The Gaze of Orpheus*. New York: Station Hill, 1981.

[3] This way of operating refers us to the urban techniques of working that were born from the surrealists and developed at the hands of the *situationist international*, one of the most influential ideological associations of the 1968. the *situationists* believed that the only way to reach against the modern bureaucratic stance and the *society of spectacle* was to generate situations or events that could force us to re-estabilish emotional contact (*desire*) with our surroundings.

They experimented within *psychogeography*, a mediating epistemology between subject and object – a science of feelings. "*Psychogeography* is the study of precise laws and specifics effects in the geographic environment, organized consciously or unconsciously on the basis of emotions and the behaviour of individuals". Guy Debord. "*Introduction to a Critique of Urban Geography*". In Ken Knabb. *Situationist International Anthology*. Berkeley, Ca: Bureau of Public Secrets, 1981.

A. Zaera, *Jean Nouvel. Intensifying the Real*, in *El Croquis*, 65/66, 1994 pp. 47-49.

Bibliography

G. Fessy, J. Nouvel, H. Tonka, *Institut du Monde Arabe*, Champ Vallon, Paris 1988.

J. Budrillard, J. Nouvel, *The Singular Object of Architecture*, University of Minnesota Press, Minneapolis 2002.

P. Goulet, *Jean Nouvel*, Electa, Paris 1987.

M. Vitard, C. Barto, B. Barto, *Onyx De la Villette… De Saint-Herblain*, Les Editions du Demi-cercle, Paris 1990.

O. Boissière, G. Fessy, *L'INIST dans l'oeuvre de Jean Nouvel*, Les Editions du Demi-cercle, Paris 1992.

H. Tonka, J.M. Sens, *Le Bateau Ivre*, Sense & Tonka editeurs, Paris 1994.

Jean Nouvel, "Expanden Version", *El Croquis*, 65/66, Madrid 1994.

The Unbuilt, Jean Nouvel, 100 Unbuilt Projects, Kenchiku Bunka, 1996.

AA.VV, *Jean Nouvel – Una lezione italiana*, Skira Editore, Milan 1996.

C.L. Morgan, Jean Nouvel, *The Elements of Architecture*, Thames & Hudson, London 1998.

F. Cirillo, *Saper credere in Architettura. Tre domande a Jean Nouvel*, Clean Edizioni, Naples 1998.

Jean Nouvel, exhibit catalogue, Editions Centre Georges Pompidou, Paris 2001.

Jean Nouvel, *El Croquis*, 112/113, Madrid 2003.

Jean Nouvel, *And*, Florence 2003.

O. Boissière, *Jean Nouvel*, Rusconi libri per Idea Libri, Santarcangelo di Romagna 2003 (Italian edition ed. Artemisa progetti editoriali).

Jean Nouvel, *Guthrie Theater – Musée du Quai Branly*, Detail Japan, Tokyo 2006.

Jean Nouvel, *Area*, 89, 2006.

Jean Nouvel 1997-2006, "A+U", 2006.

"Jean Nouvel - 3 buildings - Quai Branly Museum, Guthrie Theater, Extension of Reina Sofia Museum", *GA Document*, Tokyo 2006.